TOP DOWNLOADS

CONTENTS

Ukulele by
Chris Kringel

ISBN 978-1-4803-9043-0

HAL•LEONARD®
CORPORATION
7777 W. BLUEMOUND RD. P.O. BOX 13819 MILWAUKEE, WI 53213

Visit Hal Leonard Online at
www.halleonard.com

All of Me

Words and Music by John Stephens and Toby Gad

TRACK 1

First note
×××

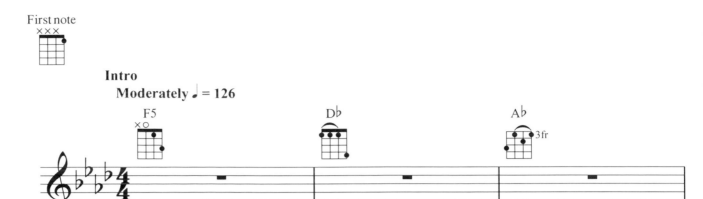

Intro
Moderately ♩ = 126

1. What would I do with-out your smart
2. How man-y times do I have to tell

mouth draw-in' me in and you kick-ing me out? __
you, e - ven when you're cry-ing, you're beau-ti-ful too? __

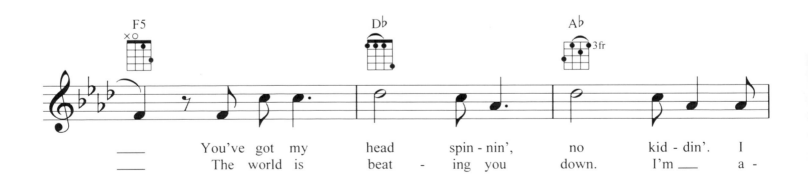

__ You've got my head spin-nin', no kid-din'. I
__ The world is beat - ing you down. I'm __ a -

can't   pin you   down.   What's go - in'
round   through ev - er - y mood. _____   You're ___ my

on in that beau - ti - ful   mind? _____   I'm on your
down - fall, you're my   muse, _____   my worst ___ dis - trac -

mag - i - cal mys - ter - y ride. _____   And   I'm
- tion, my rhy - thm and blues. _____   I can't stop

so   diz - zy; don't know what hit me. But   I'll   be al -
sing - in', ___   it's ring - in' in _____ my   head ___ for you.___

Pre-Chorus

___ right.   My head's un - der wa - ter, _____ but I'm ___

___ breath - ing fine. _____   You're ___ cra - zy and I'm ___

3

Brave

Words and Music by Sara Bareilles and Jack Antonoff

TRACK 3

_____ sun-light. _ Some-times a shad-ow wins. But I

§ Chorus

won-der what would hap-pen if you say what you wan-na say
Say what you wan-na say
* 2nd time tacet for 8 measures.

and let the words fall out hon-est-ly.

I wan-na see you be brave _____ with what you wan-na say

and let the words fall out hon-est-ly. I wan-na see you be brave.

I just wan-na see you, I just wan-na see you, _ I

8

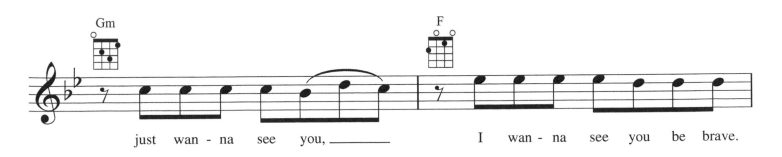

just wan-na see you, _____ I wan-na see you be brave.

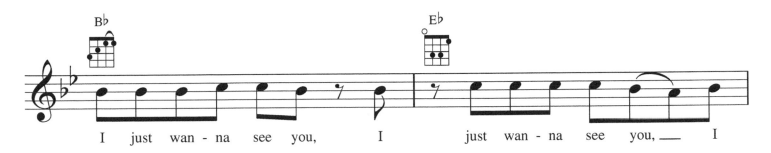

I just wan-na see you, I just wan-na see you, ___ I

To Coda ⊕ F   N.C.

just wan-na see you, _____ I wan-na see you be brave. ___

Verse

2. Ev-'ry-bod-y's been there, ev-'ry-bod-y's been stared _ down by the en-e-my. _

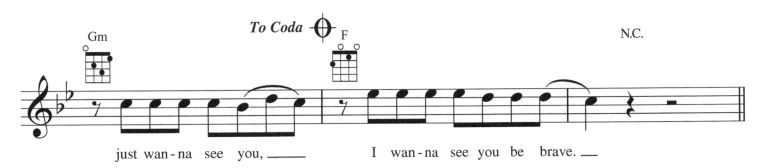

_____ Fall-en for the fear and done some dis-ap-pear-in', bow down to the might-y.

Don't ___ run, just stop hold-in' your tongue.

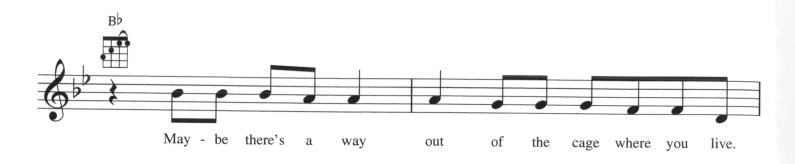

May - be there's a way out of the cage where you live.

May - be one of these days __ you can let the light __ in and show __ me

Chorus

how big your brave __ is. Say what you wan - na say and let the words fall

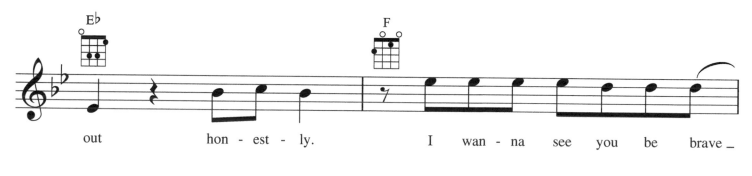

out hon - est - ly. I wan - na see you be brave __

__ with what you wan - na say and let the words fall out hon - est - ly.

Bridge

I wan - na see you be brave. _____ And ___ since your ___

Get Lucky

Words and Music by Thomas Bangalter, Guy Manuel Homem Christo, Pharrell Williams and Nile Rodgers

who we are. ____ So, let's raise the bar ____

and our cups ____ to the stars. ____

Chorus

She's up ____ all night ____ till the sun, I'm up ____ all night ____ to get some.

She's up ____ all night ____ for good fun, I'm up ____ all night ____ to get ____ luck - y.

We're up ____ all night ____ till the sun, we're up ____ all night ____ to get some.

To Coda 2

We're up ____ all night ____ for good fun, we're up ____ all night ____ to get luck - y.

We're up ___ all night ___ to get luck-y, we're up ___ all night ___ to get luck-y,

To Coda 1

we're up ___ all night ___ to get luck-y, we're up ___ all night ___ to get luck-y.

Interlude

D.S. al Coda 1

2. The pres-ent has ___ no rib -

Coda 1

*(We're up   all night   to get,   we're up   all night   to get,
*Processed w/vocoder (next 16 meas).

we're up   all night   to get,   we're up   all night   to get.

We're up   all night   to   get   to-geth - er,   all night to get to-geth-

Let Her Go

Words and Music by Michael David Rosenberg

TRACK 7

sun when it starts to snow. ___ On - ly know you love her when you let her go.

On - ly know ___ you've been high when you're feel-ing low. On - ly hate the

To Coda ⊕

road when you're miss-ing home. ___ On - ly know you love her when you let her go.

1. D Dsus4 D | 2. D Dsus4 D **Interlude** Em Cmaj7

And you let her go, _____ oh, _____ oh, no. ___

And you let her go, _____ oh, _____ oh, ___ no. ___

Well, you let her go. _____

18

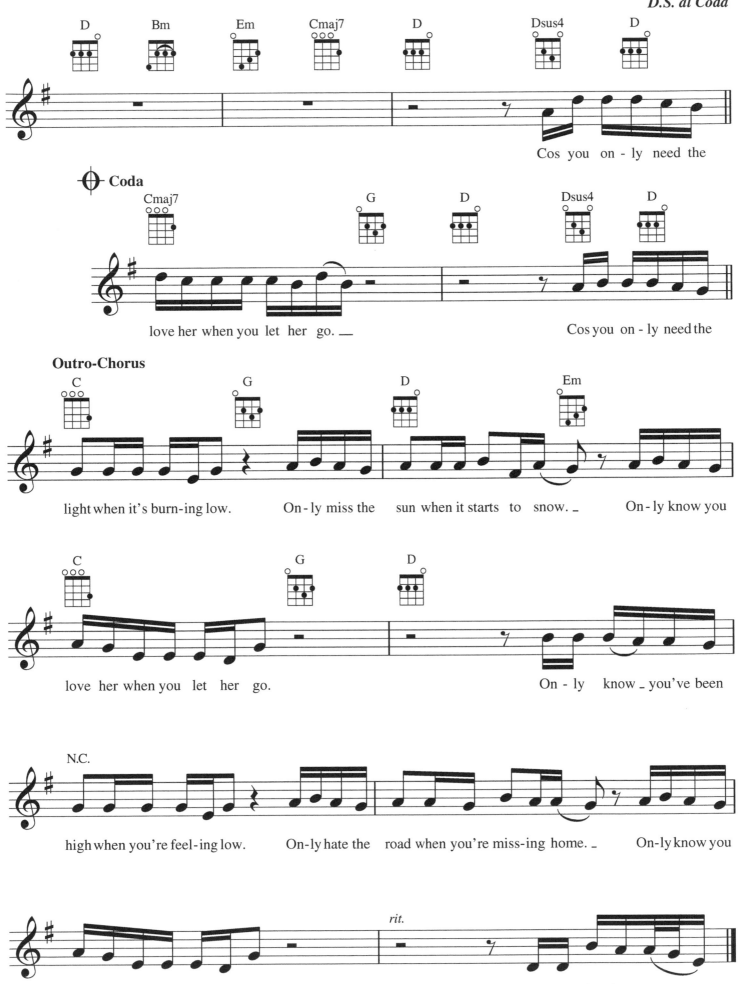

Let It Go

from Disney's Animated Feature FROZEN
Music and Lyrics by Kristen Anderson-Lopez and Robert Lopez

TRACK 9

don't let ___ them see; be the good girl you

al - ways have ___ to be. Con - ceal, ___ don't feel,

don't let ___ them know... ___ Well, now

.𝄋 Chorus

___ they know. ___ Let it go, ___ let it go; ___
let it go; ___

can't ___ hold it back an - y - more. ___ Let it go, ___
I am one with the wind and sky. ___ Let it go, ___

let it go; ___ turn a - way ___
let it go; ___ you'll ___ nev -

22

fears that once ___ con - trolled ___ me can't

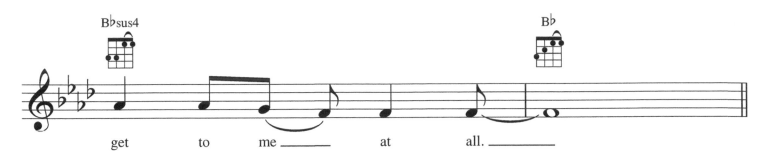

get to me ___ at all. ___

Pre-Chorus

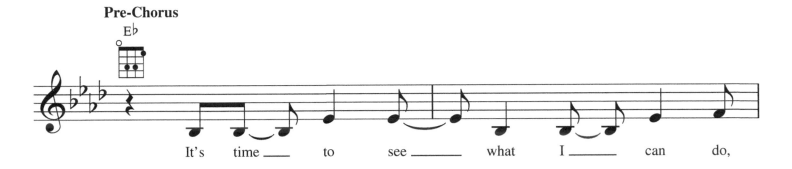

It's time ___ to see ___ what I ___ can do,

to test ___ the lim - its and ___ break through. ___

___ No right, ___ no wrong, ___ no rules ___ for me, ___

N.C. ***D.S. al Coda***

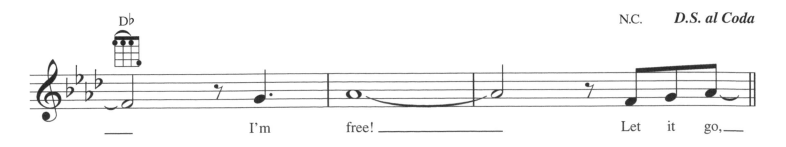

___ I'm free! _____ Let it go, ___

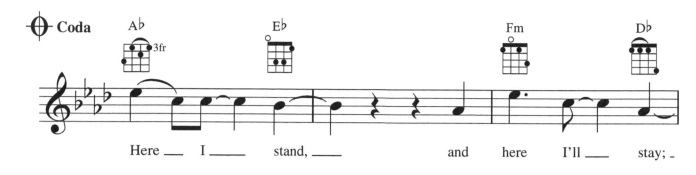

Coda

Here — I — stand, — and here I'll — stay; —

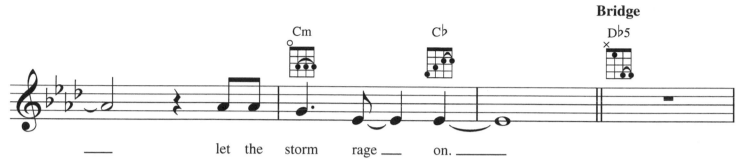

Bridge

— let the storm rage — on. —

My pow - er flur -

- ries through — the air — in - to — the ground. —

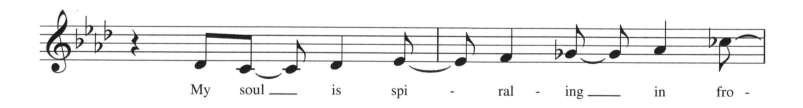

My soul — is spi - ral - ing — in fro -

- zen frac - tals all — a - round. —

And one _____ thought cry - stal - li - zes like _____

_____ an i - cy blast: _____

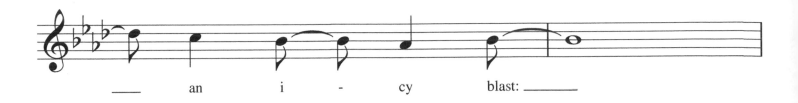

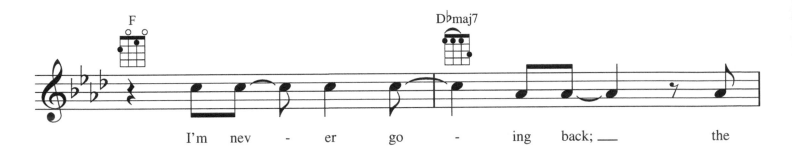

I'm nev - er go - ing back; _____ the

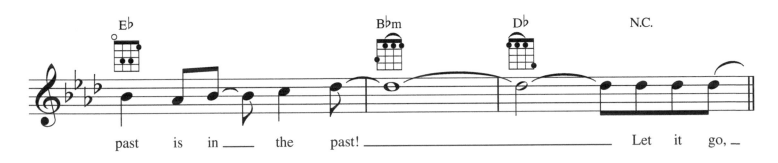

past is in _____ the past! _____ Let it go, _

Chorus

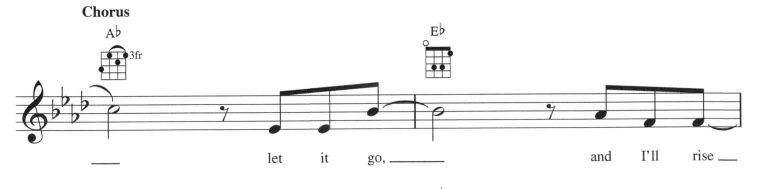

_____ let it go, _____ and I'll rise _

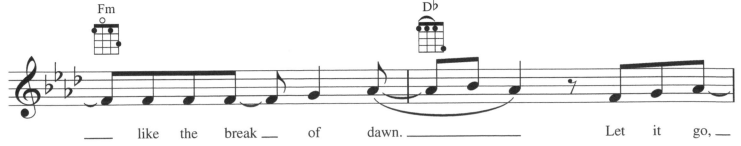

_____ like the break _ of dawn. _____ Let it go, _

let it go; _____ that per-

-fect girl _____ is _____ gone. _____

Here _____ I _____ stand _____ in the

light _____ of _____ day; _____

_____ let the storm rage ___ on. _____ The

cold nev - er both - ered me an - y - way.

Roar

Words and Music by Katy Perry, Lukasz Gottwald, Max Martin, Bonnie McKee and Henry Walter

TRACK 11

First note

Intro
Moderately slow ♩ = 90

Verse

1. I used to bite my tongue and hold — my breath, scared to rock the boat and make — a mess.

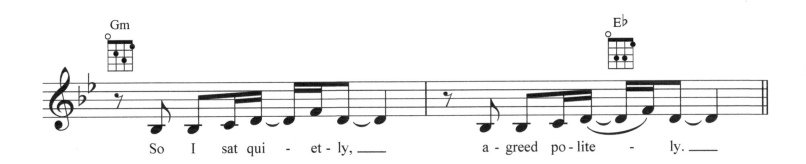

So I sat qui - et - ly, ___ a - greed po - lite - ly. ___

I guess that I for-got I had — a choice. I let you push me past the break - ing point.
2. Now I'm float-in' like a but - ter - fly. Sting-in' like a bee, I earned — my stripes.

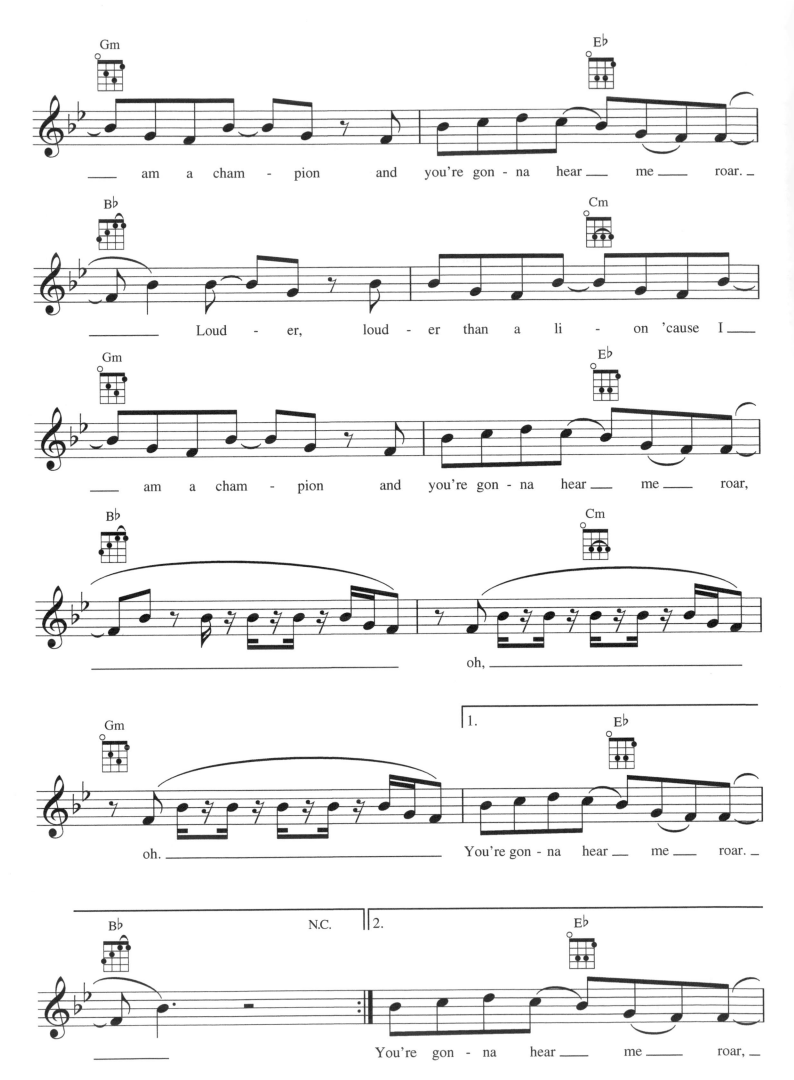

am a cham - pion and you're gon - na hear __ me __ roar. __

__ Loud - er, loud - er than a li - on 'cause I __

__ am a cham - pion and you're gon - na hear __ me __ roar,

oh, __

oh. __ You're gon - na hear __ me __ roar. __

You're gon - na hear __ me __ roar,

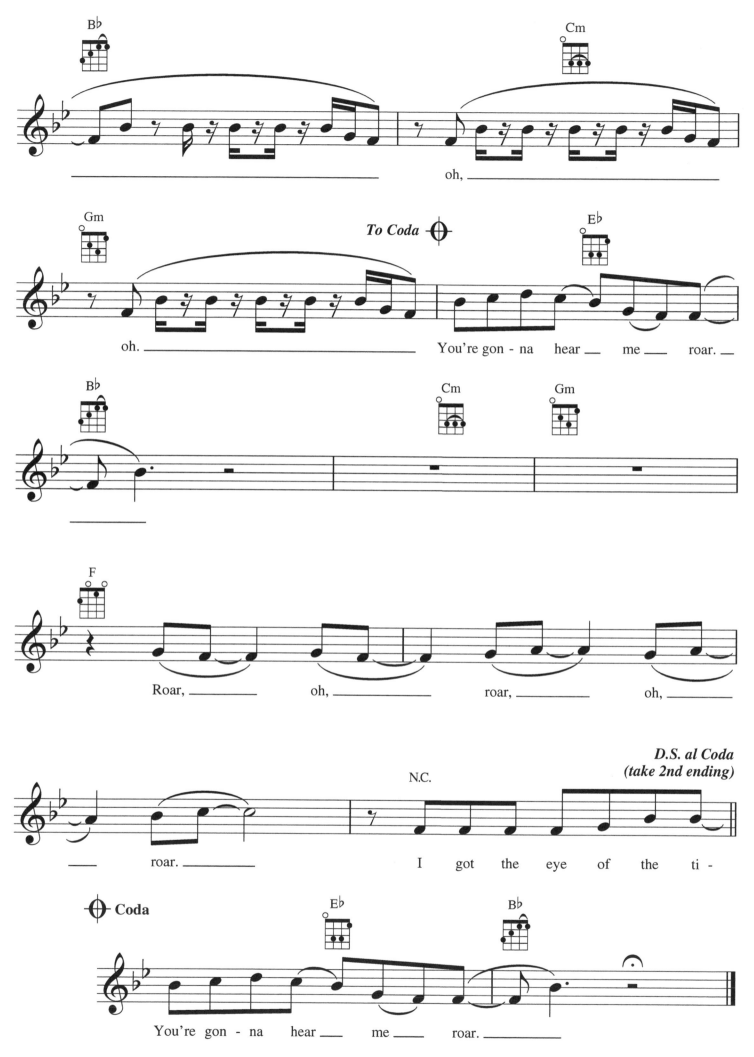

Say Something

Words and Music by Ian Axel, Chad Vaccarino and Mike Campbell

Say some-thing, I'm giv-ing up on you.

I'll be the one if you want me to.

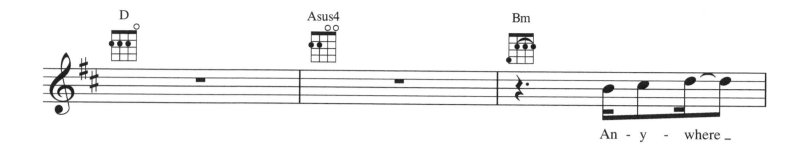

An - y - where _

I would have fol - lowed you. __

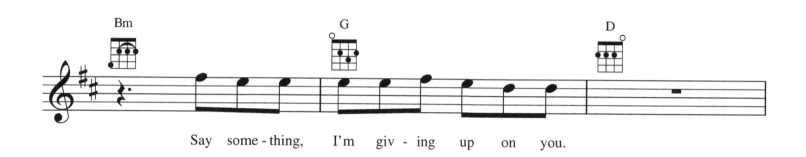

Say some - thing, I'm giv - ing up on you.

Verse

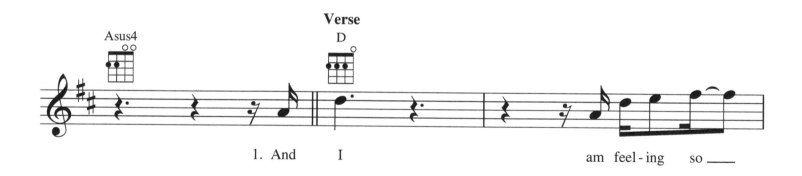

1. And I am feel - ing so ____

small. It was o - ver my head;

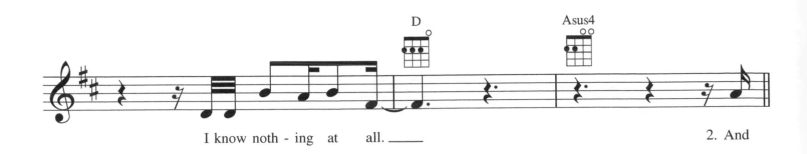

I know noth - ing at all. _____

2. And

Verse

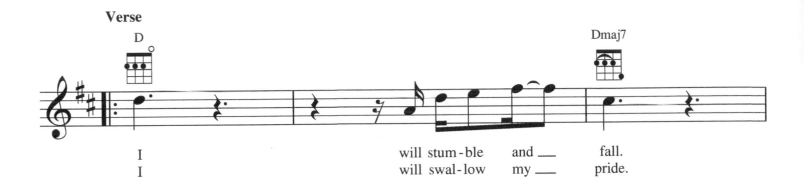

I

I will stum - ble and __ fall.
will swal - low my __ pride.

I'm still learn - ing to love,
You're the one that I love,

just start - ing to crawl. _
and I'm say - ing good-bye. __

Chorus

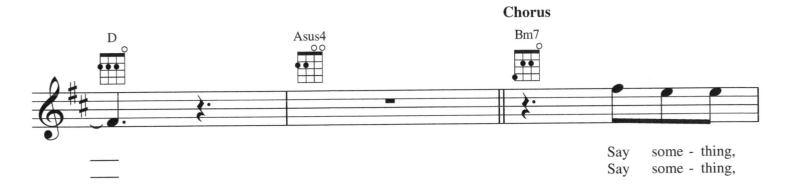

__
__

Say some - thing,
Say some - thing,

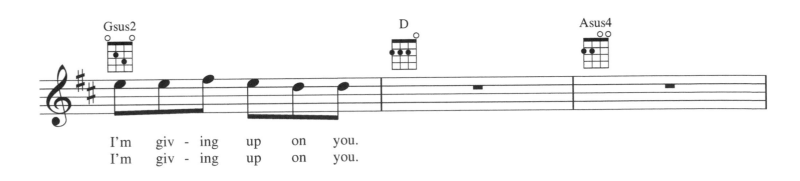

I'm giv - ing up on you.
I'm giv - ing up on you.

34

I'm sor - ry that I _____ could-n't get ___ to you. ___
And I'm sor - ry that I _____ could-n't get ___ to you. ___

An - y - where } I would have fol - lowed you. _
And an - y - where }

Say some - thing, I'm giv - ing up on you.

1.   2.

3. And

Say some - thing, I'm giv - ing up on you.

Say some - thing.

Royals

Words and Music by Ella Yelich-O'Connor and Joel Little

First note

Moderately slow ♩ = 85

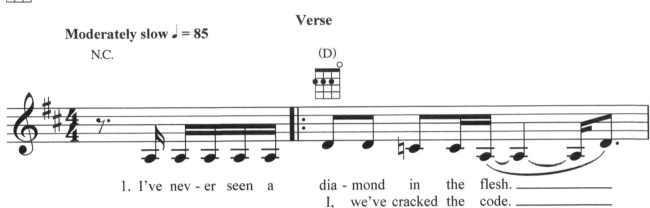

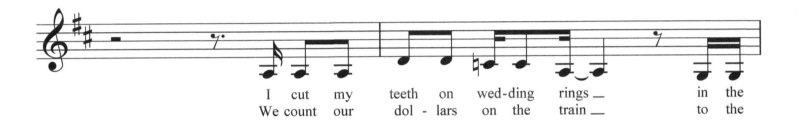

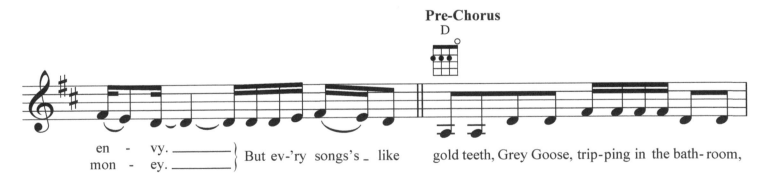

bloodstains, ball gowns, trash-ing the ho-tel room. We don't care, __ we're driv-in'

Cad-il-lacs in our dreams. __ But ev-'ry-bod-y's like Crys-tal, May-bach, dia-monds on your time-piece,

jet planes, is-lands, ti-gers on a gold leash. We don't care, __ we aren't

𝄋 **Chorus**

caught up in your love af-fair. __ And we'll nev-er be roy-als. (Roy-als.)

It don't run in our __ blood. _ That kind of luxe just ain't __ for us. __ We crave a

dif-f'rent kind __ of buzz. __ Let me be __ your rul-er. (Rul-er.)

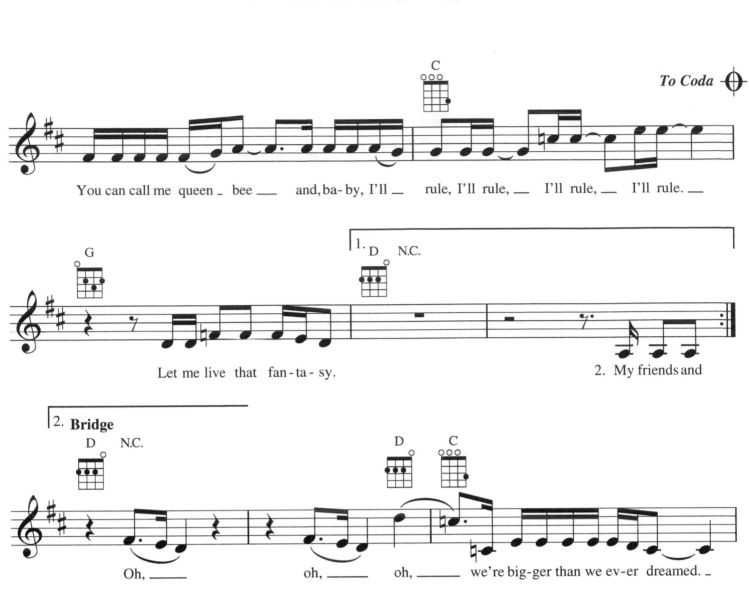

You can call me queen _ bee _ and, ba-by, I'll _ rule, I'll rule, _ I'll rule, _ I'll rule. _

Let me live that fan-ta-sy.

1. 2. My friends and

2. **Bridge**

Oh, _ oh, _ oh, _ we're big-ger than we ev-er dreamed. _

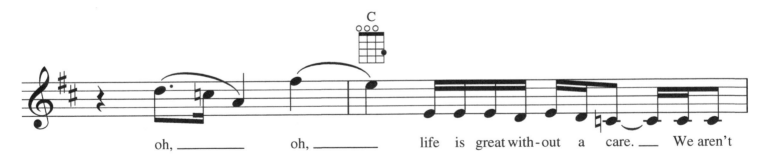

And I'm in love with be-ing queen. _ Oh, _

oh, _ oh, _ life is great with-out a care. _ We aren't

D.S. al Coda Coda

caught up in your love af-fair. _ And we'll nev-er be

Let me live that fan-ta-sy.

UKULELE NOTATION LEGEND

THE MUSICAL STAFF shows pitches and rhythms and is divided by bar lines into measures. Pitches are named after the first seven letters of the alphabet.

TABLATURE graphically represents the ukulele fingerboard. Each horizontal line represents a a string, and each number represents a fret.

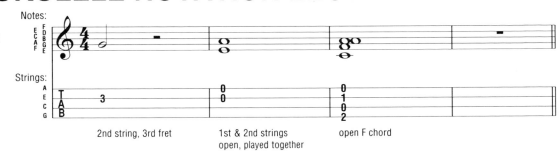

2nd string, 3rd fret   1st & 2nd strings open, played together   open F chord

HALF-STEP BEND: Strike the note and bend up 1/2 step.

WHOLE-STEP BEND: Strike the note and bend up one step.

GRACE NOTE BEND: Strike the note and immediately bend up as indicated.

SLIGHT (MICROTONE) BEND: Strike the note and bend up 1/4 step.

BEND AND RELEASE: Strike the note and bend up as indicated, then release back to the original note. Only the first note is struck.

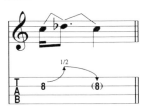

PRE-BEND: Bend the note as indicated, then strike it.

VIBRATO: The string is vibrated by rapidly bending and releasing the note with the fretting hand.

HAMMER-ON: Strike the first (lower) note with one finger, then sound the higher note (on the same string) with another finger by fretting it without picking.

PULL-OFF: Place both fingers on the notes to be sounded. Strike the first note and without picking, pull the finger off to sound the second (lower) note.

LEGATO SLIDE: Strike the first note and then slide the same fret-hand finger up or down to the second note. The second note is not struck.

SHIFT SLIDE: Same as legato slide, except the second note is struck.

TRILL: Very rapidly alternate between the notes indicated by continuously hammering on and pulling off.

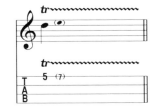

TREMOLO PICKING: The note is picked as rapidly and continuously as possible.

NOTE: Tablature numbers in parentheses mean:

1. The note is being sustained over a system (note in standard notation is tied), or

2. The note is sustained, but a new articulation (such as a hammer-on, pull-off, slide or vibrato) begins, or

3. The note is a barely audible "ghost" note (note in standard notation is also in parentheses).

Additional Musical Definitions

    (accent) — • Accentuate note (play it louder)

   (staccato) — • Play the note short

D.S. al Coda — • Go back to the sign (𝄋), then play until the measure marked "**To Coda**," then skip to the section labelled "**Coda**."

D.C. al Fine — • Go back to the beginning of the song and play until the measure marked "**Fine**" (end).

N.C. — • No chord.

 — • Repeat measures between signs.

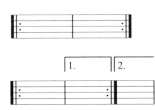 — • When a repeated section has different endings, play the first ending only the first time and the second ending only the second time.

HAL•LEONARD® UKULELE PLAY-ALONG

AUDIO ACCESS INCLUDED

Now you can play your favorite songs on your uke with great-sounding backing tracks to help you sound like a bona fide pro! The audio also features playback tools so you can adjust the tempo without changing the pitch and loop challenging parts.

1. POP HITS
00701451 Book/CD Pack $15.99

2. UKE CLASSICS
00701452 Book/CD Pack $15.99

3. HAWAIIAN FAVORITES
00701453 Book/Online Audio $14.99

4. CHILDREN'S SONGS
00701454 Book/Online Audio $14.99

5. CHRISTMAS SONGS
00701696 Book/CD Pack $12.99

6. LENNON & MCCARTNEY
00701723 Book/Online Audio $12.99

7. DISNEY FAVORITES
00701724 Book/Online Audio $12.99

8. CHART HITS
00701745 Book/CD Pack $15.99

9. THE SOUND OF MUSIC
00701784 Book/CD Pack $14.99

10. MOTOWN
00701964 Book/CD Pack $12.99

11. CHRISTMAS STRUMMING
00702458 Book/Online Audio $12.99

12. BLUEGRASS FAVORITES
00702584 Book•CD Pack $12.99

13. UKULELE SONGS
00702599 Book/CD Pack $12.99

14. JOHNNY CASH
00702615 Book/CD Pack $15.99

15. COUNTRY CLASSICS
00702834 Book/CD Pack $12.99

16. STANDARDS
00702835 Book/CD Pack $12.99

17. POP STANDARDS
00702836 Book/CD Pack $12.99

18. IRISH SONGS
00703086 Book/Online Audio $12.99

19. BLUES STANDARDS
00703087 Book/CD Pack $12.99

20. FOLK POP ROCK
00703088 Book/CD Pack $12.99

21. HAWAIIAN CLASSICS
00703097 Book/CD Pack $12.99

22. ISLAND SONGS
00703098 Book/CD Pack $12.99

23. TAYLOR SWIFT – 2ND EDITION
00221966 Book/Online Audio $16.99

24. WINTER WONDERLAND
00101871 Book/CD Pack $12.99

25. GREEN DAY
00110398 Book/CD Pack $14.99

26. BOB MARLEY
00110399 Book/Online Audio $14.99

27. TIN PAN ALLEY
00116358 Book/CD Pack $12.99

28. STEVIE WONDER
00116736 Book/CD Pack $14.99

29. OVER THE RAINBOW & OTHER FAVORITES
00117076 Book/Online Audio $14.99

30. ACOUSTIC SONGS
00122336 Book/CD Pack $14.99

31. JASON MRAZ
00124166 Book/CD Pack $14.99

32. TOP DOWNLOADS
00127507 Book/CD Pack $14.99

33. CLASSICAL THEMES
00127892 Book/Online Audio $14.99

34. CHRISTMAS HITS
00128602 Book/CD Pack $14.99

35. SONGS FOR BEGINNERS
00129009 Book/Online Audio $14.99

36. ELVIS PRESLEY HAWAII
00138199 Book/Online Audio $14.99

37. LATIN
00141191 Book/Online Audio $14.99

38. JAZZ
00141192 Book/Online Audio $14.99

39. GYPSY JAZZ
00146559 Book/Online Audio $14.99

40. TODAY'S HITS
00160845 Book/Online Audio $14.99

Prices, contents, and availability
subject to change without notice.

HAL•LEONARD®
www.halleonard.com